Let's Write!

Realistic Fiction

15 min.

You will need
- paper
- pencil

● Write a realistic story about an unexpected event. Give details about the characters and setting and tell what happens. Use vivid words.

▲ Write a realistic story about an unexpected event. Use vivid words to describe the characters and setting. Tell what happens to the characters.

■ Write a realistic story about an unexpected event. Use vivid words to describe the characters and setting and tell what happens. Proofread for word choice.

Let's Write!

Dramatic Scene

15 min.

You will need
- paper
- pencils

● Think of a situation that could happen unexpectedly. Write a dramatic scene with two characters in this situation. Write dialogue that shows what happens.

▲ Write a dramatic scene about two people in an unexpected situation. Write realistic dialogue that explains what happens to the characters. Proofread for wordiness.

■ Write a dramatic scene that shows what happens when two people are placed in an unexpected situation. Write realistic dialogue with stage directions that explains what happens to the characters. Proofread for wordiness.

Let's Write!

Realistic Fiction

You will need
- paper
- pencil

15 min.

● Write a realistic story about two characters who travel somewhere. Tell where the characters go and how they travel. Tell what happens when they arrive.

▲ Write a realistic story with two characters who travel to a place they want to visit. Explain where they are going and what happens when they arrive.

■ Write a realistic story about two characters traveling to a place they want to visit. Include details explaining where they are going, how they get there, and what happens when they arrive.

Let's Write!

Skit

15 min.

You will need
- paper
- pencils

● Think of something you recently learned how to do. Write a short skit that shows one character teaching another how to do this. Write dialogue with vivid words.

▲ Write a skit that shows one character teaching another character how to do something. Write dialogue that includes vivid words. Proofread your skit and focus on word choice.

■ Write a skit showing one character teaching another how to do something. Include dialogue that uses vivid words and write stage directions that show action. Proofread for word choice.

Let's Write!

Expository Composition

15 min.

You will need
- paper
- pencil

● Think about a job that interests you. Write an expository composition that tells about a job you would like to have. Describe what you would do. Organize your ideas around a main idea.

▲ Write an expository composition about a job that interests you. Explain the responsibilities of the job. Organize your ideas around a main idea.

■ Write an expository composition describing a job you would like to have. Explain the responsibilities of this job and how you would get the job.

Let's Write!

Book Review

15 min.

You will need
- paper
- pencils

● Think about a book you read recently. Write a review that tells your opinion of the book. Include details that would be helpful to readers. Begin your sentences with a variety of words.

▲ Write a review of a book you read recently. Give your opinion of the book and include plot details. Use a variety of words to begin your sentences.

■ Write a review that gives your opinion of a book you read recently. Include interesting details about the plot and explain why it might interest others. Vary your sentence beginnings.

Let's Write!

Parody

You will need
- paper
- pencil

15 min.

● Work with a partner to think of a story that you both know well. Write a parody of the story. Use similar characters and story details as the original story.

▲ Work with a partner to write a parody of a popular story. Use a humorous voice and include details that are similar to the original story.

■ Work with a partner to write a parody of a story you know well. Include characters and details that are similar to the original story. Be sure to add funny twists.

Let's Write!

Cause-and-Effect Essay

15 min.

You will need
- paper
- pencils

● Think about a problem in your community. Write a cause-and-effect essay about the problem. Write two sentences about the cause of the problem. Write two sentences about the effects.

▲ Write a cause-and-effect essay about a problem in your community. Write a short paragraph about the cause of the problem and a short paragraph about the effects of the problem.

■ Choose a problem in your community, and write a cause-and-effect essay explaining the problem. Write a paragraph describing the cause of the problem. Write a paragraph stating the effects.

 Grade 4, Unit 6, Week 2

27

Let's Write!

Friendly Letter

You will need
- paper
- pencil

15 min.

● Write a friendly letter to someone describing something you've done recently. Give details about the event. Use a comma in your greeting and your closing.

▲ Write a friendly letter to someone describing something fun you have done recently. Tell why you enjoyed the event. Use commas in the salutation and closing. Check punctuation.

■ Write a friendly letter describing an event you have been to recently. Include details explaining why the event was fun. Proofread your letter for punctuation and proper use of commas.

Let's Write!

Personal Narrative

15 min.

You will need
- paper
- pencils

● Think about a time something unexpected happened to you. Write a personal story telling about this time. Explain why the event was unexpected. Use smooth sentence flow.

▲ Write a personal narrative about a time something unexpected happened to you. Explain what you thought was going to happen. Give details about what did happen. Proofread for sentence flow.

■ Write a personal narrative with several details about a time something unexpected happened to you. Explain what was supposed to happen. Proofread for sentence flow.

Let's Write!

Personal Narrative

15 min.

You will need
- paper
- pencil

● Write a personal narrative describing an unexpected event. Include details telling why it was unexpected.

▲ Write a personal narrative about something unexpected that happened to you. Explain why the event was unexpected. Use a voice that engages your audience.

■ Write a personal narrative describing an unexpected event you experienced. Give details explaining why it was unexpected. Use a voice that reflects the tone of your writing.

Let's Write!

Persuasive Advertisement

15 min.

You will need
- paper
- pencils

● Think of a place you like to visit. Write a persuasive ad convincing people to visit this place. Explain why they should visit. Draw a picture to go with your ad.

▲ Think of a place you like to visit and write a persuasive ad convincing other why they should visit. Include one or two details explaining why this place is great. Draw a picture to go with your ad.

■ Write a persuasive ad convincing others to visit one of your favorite places. Focus on details explaining why this place is special. Draw a picture to display with your ad.

Humorous Limerick

You will need
- paper
- pencil

15 min.

● Write a limerick about a funny person, place, or thing. Include an example of alliteration or onomatopoeia in your limerick.

▲ Write a limerick about a person, place, or thing. Include at least one example of alliteration or onomatopoeia in your limerick. Proofread for proper rhyme scheme.

■ Write a limerick about a person, place, or thing. Include one example of alliteration and one of onomatopoeia. Choose humorous words and proofread for proper rhyme scheme.

Thank-You Note

15 min.

You will need
- paper
- pencils

● Think of something nice someone has done for you recently. Write a thank-you note to the person. Tell them why you are thankful. Choose exact words to help make the purpose of your note clear.

▲ Write a thank-you letter to someone who has helped you recently. Explain why you are thankful to this person and choose exact words that clarify the purpose of your note.

■ Write a thank-you letter expressing your gratitude for something someone has done for you recently. Choose exact words that help clarify the purpose of your letter. Proofread for word choice.

Let's Write!

News Article

15 min.

You will need
- paper
- pencil

● Think about something that happened recently in your community. Write a news article about the event. Include facts and details to help explain the event.

▲ Write an article about something that happened recently in your community. Include facts and details that help explain the event. Focus your ideas on information that will inform your audience.

■ Write a news article that tells about a recent event in your community. Focus your ideas and include facts and details that will inform your audience.

Let's Write!

Legend

You will need
- paper
- pencils

15 min.

● Think about a famous person from history. Write a legend about this person. Include interesting facts that tell about this person. Proofread your legend.

▲ Think about a famous person from history. Write a legend about this person that gives interesting facts and details. Proofread and combine short sentences.

■ Think of a famous person from history. Write a legend about this person's life. Include interesting details and explain the reason the person is famous. Combine short, choppy sentences.

Free-Verse Poem

You will need

• paper   • pencil

15 min.

● Write a poem about a real person or a character in a story. Use one simile to describe the person or character. Proofread your poem.

▲ Write a poem about a real person or a story character. Use at least one simile to describe the person or character. Proofread your poem for organization and word choice.

■ Write a poem describing a real-life person or character in a story. Use similes in your descriptions. Proofread your poem's organization and word choice.

Let's Write!

Fantasy

15 min.

You will need
- paper
- pencils

● Imagine that you met a person from another planet. Write a short fantasy telling about the meeting. Explain why the person was visiting Earth. Proofread your work for complete sentences.

▲ Write a fantasy about meeting a person from another planet. Include details explaining the person's reasons for visiting Earth. Check punctuation and use complete sentences.

■ Write a fantasy about meeting a person from another planet. Include details explaining what brings the person to Earth. Proofread for capitalization and punctuation.

Let's Write!

Directions

15 min.

You will need
- paper
- pencils

● Write directions that tell how to get from your classroom to another location in your school. Number each step. Include important details such as *turn left* or *turn right*.

▲ Write directions that explain how to complete a task, such as how to prepare a sandwich. Number each step and include a list of supplies you will need to complete the task.

■ Write step-by-step directions telling how to complete a task. Include details, such as the materials you will need for the task. Write a topic sentence and organize the directions into steps.

Fictional Adventure

15 min.

You will need
- paper
- pencils

● Imagine a character on an adventure that takes place in the past. Write about the character and his or her adventure. Give details about the adventure in the plot.

▲ Write about an adventure that takes place in the past. Include a character in your adventure and give details in the plot explaining what happens. Proofread your story for strong, active verbs.

■ Write an adventure story set in the past. Give details about the character and plot and describe what happens to the character. Proofread to make sure you have used strong, active verbs.

Let's Write!

Persuasive Article

15 min.

You will need
- paper
- pencils

● Think about the most important news story of last year. Write a persuasive article convincing others of your views about the story. Include facts and details that support your opinion.

▲ Think about the most important news story of last year. Write a persuasive article convincing others to agree with your opinion. Include facts and details that support your opinion.

■ Write a persuasive article about why you think one news story of last year is the most important. Include facts and details that support your opinion. Proofread for transitions.

Let's Write!

Problem-Solution Essay

15 min.

You will need
- paper
- pencils

● Think of a problem in your school or community. Write a problem-solution essay explaining the problem and suggesting a solution. Include important details, such as when the problem began.

▲ Write a problem-solution essay about a problem in your community. Give details explaining the problem. Describe your solution. Include all the essential information.

■ Write a problem-solution essay about an issue in your community. Provide details about the problem and how to solve it. Include all the essential information.

Let's Write!

Narrative Poem

15 min.

You will need
- paper
- pencils

● Think of a person who has accomplished many things. Write a narrative poem about this person. Give your poem a rhythm that follows a pattern. Proofread for rhythm.

▲ Write a narrative poem about a historical figure. Include details that describe the person. Give your poem a rhythm that follows a pattern. Proofread for rhythm.

■ Write a narrative poem about a historical figure. Write so that the poem has a rhythm that follows a pattern. Proofread your poem for organization and rhythm.

Let's Write!

Step-by-Step Instructions

15 min.

You will need
- paper
- pencils

● Think about a game you play. Write step-by-step instructions telling how to play it. Write a number followed by a colon for each step. Proofread for a complete list.

▲ Write step-by-step instructions telling how to make a snack. Write a number followed by a colon for each step. Proofread your instructions to make sure your list is complete.

■ Write step-by-step instructions telling how to complete a task. Number each step and place a colon after the number. Proofread your instructions to make sure they are complete.

Let's Write!

Invitation

15 min.

You will need
- paper
- pencils
- markers

● Write an invitation to a party celebrating a special occasion. Include details about when and where the party is. Draw a picture to go with your invitation.

▲ Write an invitation to a party celebrating a special occasion. Tell when and where the party is. Use a voice that reflects your personality. Illustrate your invitation.

■ Write an invitation to a party celebrating a special occasion. Use a voice that reflects your personality. Include important details. Customize your invitation with a drawing.

Let's Write!

Song

15 min.

You will need
- paper
- pencils

● Write a song about a place you love to visit. First, list some words describing the place. List some rhyming words. Choose vivid nouns and adjectives for your song.

▲ Write a song about a person you admire. To begin, list words to describe the person. Next to each word, write rhyming words. Write a song with vivid nouns and adjectives.

■ Write a song about one of your hobbies. To begin, list a few words that describe this hobby. Then write down some rhyming words. Use vivid nouns and adjectives in your song.

Let's Write!

Myth

15 min.

You will need
- paper
- pencils

● Write a myth that explains why the stars shine at night. Include details explaining why we are not able to see stars during the day. Use both short and long sentences.

▲ Write a myth explaining something in nature, such as why we only see stars at night. Include fictional details in your explanation. Use both simple and compound sentences.

■ Write a myth explaining a natural occurrence in nature, such as why leaves turn color in the fall. Include fictional details in your explanation. Use a variety of simple and compound sentences.

Let's Write!

Mystery

15 min.

You will need
- paper
- pencils

● Write a short mystery. Remember that a mystery story has a puzzle or secret that must be solved. Try to choose words that create rhythm and style in your story.

▲ Write a mystery about a strange event. Explain what the mystery is and write sentences with clues that reveal what happens. Choose words that give your mystery a style and rhythm.

■ Write a mystery about a strange event your character witnessed. Explain what the mystery is and give details that reveal what happens. Use word choice to give your story rhythm and style.

Formal Letter

You will need

- paper
- pencils

15 min.

● Think of an issue in your town you would like to know more about. Write a letter to the mayor asking for information. Include a salutation and closing. Proofread your letter.

▲ Write a letter to the mayor asking for information about an issue in your town. Tell what you want to know in the body of the letter. Include a salutation and closing.

■ Write a letter to the mayor asking for information about an issue in your town. Explain what information you want in the body of the letter. Include a salutation and closing.

Let's Write!

Summary

15 min.

You will need
- paper
- pencils

● Think about a book you have read. Write a summary of the book that tells the main idea and key details. Include the author and title. Proofread to correct run-on sentences.

▲ Write a summary about a book you have read that tells the main idea and key details. Include title and author information. Use simple and compound sentences.

■ Write a summary that tells the main idea and key details of a book you have read. Include author and title information. Correct any run-on sentences and mix simple and compound sentences.